Match Them
Words

Animals

By Ronald Ridout

Illustrated by Karen Tushingham

Collins
in association with
Belitha Press

Dear Adult,

Here is a series of colourful and entertaining write-in books aimed at introducing nursery and infant children of 3-6 to basic recognition of words and phrases.

The **Match Them . . . Words** books (ages 3-5) will help children to learn about their immediate environment while the **Match Them . . . Nursery Rhymes** books (ages 4-6) will enable children to discover new words within a familiar context. They will also help children who are learning the rhymes for the first time!

At first, you will need to show the child how to link the word to the picture or space, but they will soon get the idea of matching for themselves, and will enjoy doing the exercises unaided.

Within each book there is a gradual progression, so that as children gain confidence, they can tackle something a little harder. Some words and matching pictures appear in both the **Words** and **Nursery Rhymes** books – and every child will have fun spotting them and so reinforce their learning!

Ronald Ridout

First published 1988 by William Collins Sons & Co Ltd
in association with Belitha Press Limited,
31 Newington Green, London N16 9PU
Text and illustrations in this format copyright © Belitha Press 1988
Text copyright © Ronald Ridout 1988
Illustrations copyright © Karen Tushingham 1988
Art Director: Treld Bicknell   Editor: Carol Watson
ISBN 0 00 197726 1
10 9 8 7 6 5 4 3 2 1
Typesetting by Chambers Wallace, London
Printed by Purnell Book Production Limited, Paulton, England, for Imago

What are they?

a cat   a rat   a crab

Can you match the words and pictures?
Begin like this:

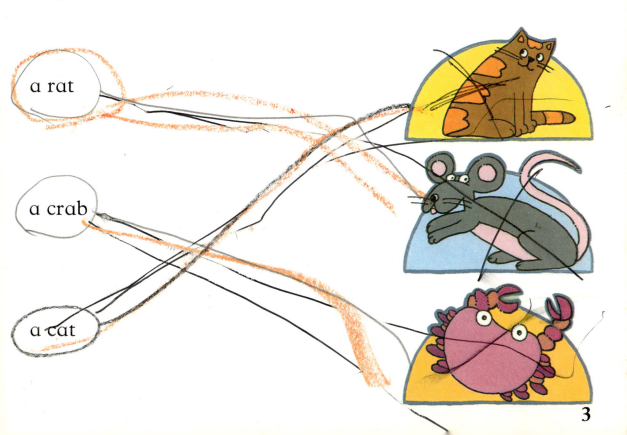

a rat

a crab

a cat

What are they?

a dog

a frog

a fish

a pig

Now match these words and pictures.
Begin like this:

a frog

a fish

a dog

a pig

Who is playing leapfrog?

What are these?

| dogs | cats | hens | birds | cows |

Match the words with the pictures.
Begin like this:

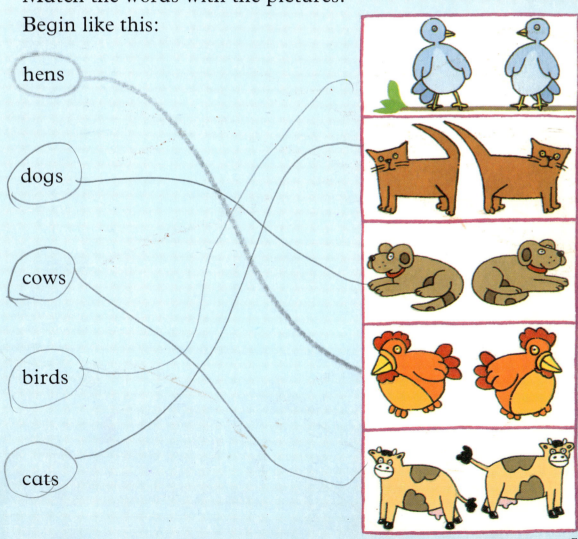

hens

dogs

cows

birds

cats

Numbers!

1	2	3	4	5
one	two	three	four	five

Can you match the words and numbers?
Begin like this:

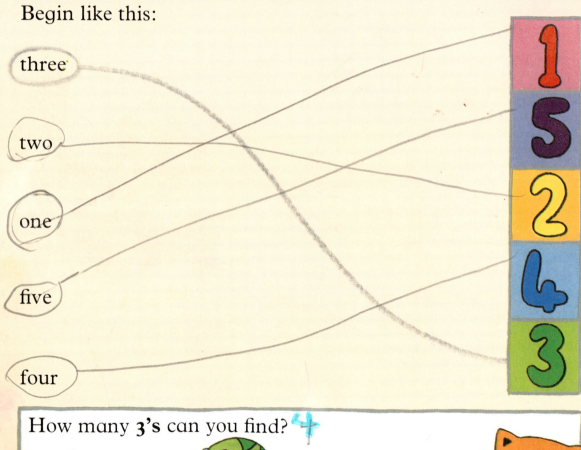

three

two

one

five

four

1
5
2
4
3

How many **3's** can you find? 4

Now match the words to the right picture. Begin like this:

two hens

five birds

one cow

four pigs

three dogs

How many cats are there? 4

What are they?

a deer   a sheep   a horse   a donkey

Match the words to the pictures. Begin like this:

a horse
a sheep
a deer

a sheep
a deer
a donkey

a deer
a donkey
a horse

Match them!

Begin like this:

- a cow
- a dog
- a sheep
- a rat
- a pig
- a donkey
- a cat
- a horse
- a deer
- a fish

Colours!

Here are some colours:

red   brown   blue

green   pink   yellow

Can you match the colours to their names? Begin like this:

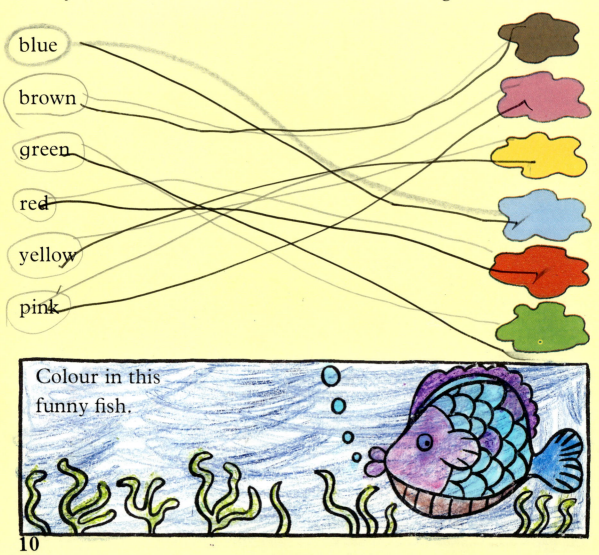

blue

brown

green

red

yellow

pink

Colour in this funny fish.

Now match the words to the pictures.
Begin like this:

a blue donkey

a green horse

a brown fish

a red frog

a yellow deer

a pink sheep

Now colour
Percy Pig.

Mothers and babies

a horse   a foal   a goat   a kid

a sheep

a lamb

a cow   a calf

a hen   a chick   a cat   a kitten

Whose baby is it?

Match the mothers to their babies. Begin like this:

a hen

a lamb

a cat

a kid

a sheep

a chick

a goat

a kitten

Name the animals
Can you read the words?

a bull

a lion

an elephant

a swan

a giraffe

a fish

a kangaroo

a rabbit

a blackbird

a hen

a monkey

an owl

What is it?

Match the sentences and the pictures. Begin like this:

It is a horse.
It is a cow.
It is a bull.
It is a monkey.

It is a goat.
It is a swan.
It is a lamb.
It is an owl.

It is a monkey.
It is a lamb.
It is a fish.
It is a lion.

How many animals?

| a spider | a ladybird | a bee | a butterfly | an ant |

Can you match the words below to the pictures?
Begin like this:

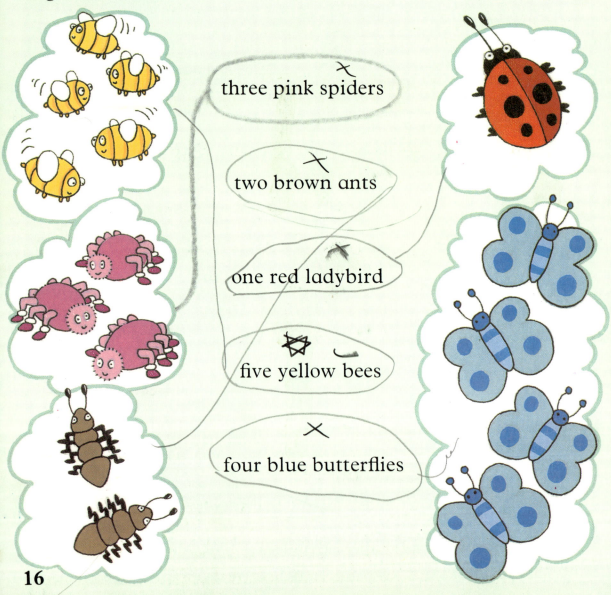

three pink spiders

two brown ants

one red ladybird

five yellow bees

four blue butterflies

What are they?

a lion

a seal

a camel

a tiger

an elephant

a crocodile

Now match these words to their pictures. Begin like this:

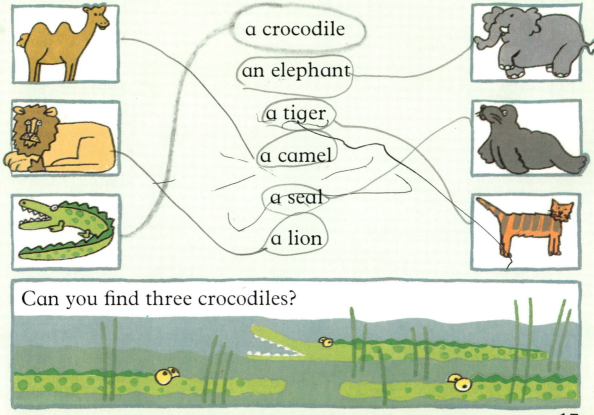

a crocodile

an elephant

a tiger

a camel

a seal

a lion

Can you find three crocodiles?

What is it?

It is a crocodile.

Can you match these sentences to the pictures?
Begin like this:

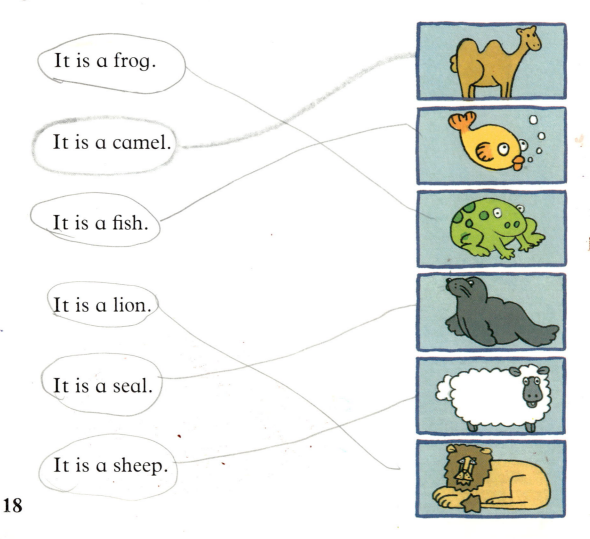

It is a frog.

It is a camel.

It is a fish.

It is a lion.

It is a seal.

It is a sheep.

Can you match the pictures to the spaces?
Begin like this:

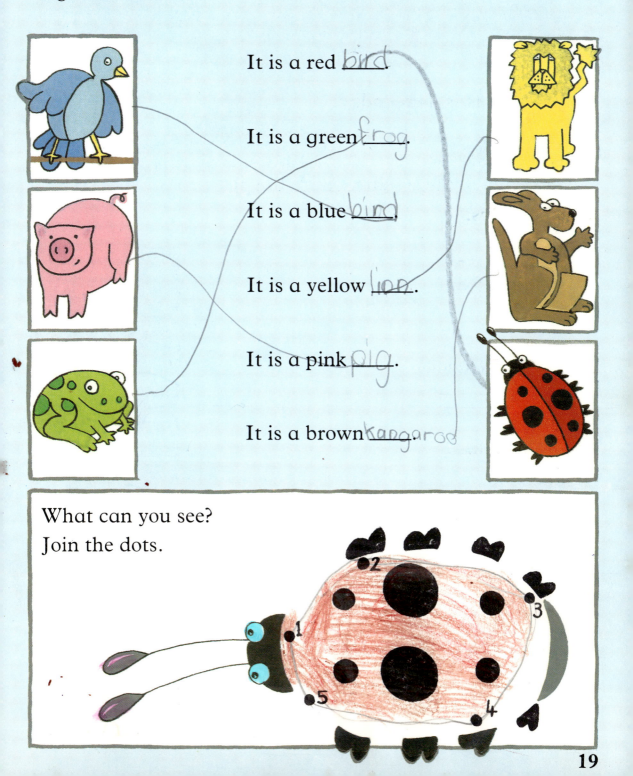

It is a red bird

It is a green frog.

It is a blue bird.

It is a yellow lion.

It is a pink pig.

It is a brown kangaroo

What can you see?
Join the dots.

What is it?

It is a cat.

Can you fill in the missing words?
Begin like this:

What is it?

It is a _pig_.

What is it?

It is a _bird_.

What is it?

It is a _goat_

pig

tiger

horse

goat

crab

bird

What is it?

It is a _horse_.

What is it?

It is a _cat_.

What is it?

It is a _crab_.

a fat cat | a thin cat | a big cat

a little cat | a happy cat | a sad cat

Can you fill in the missing words?

Begin like this:

a happy pig

a fat pig

a sad pig

fat

big

thin

happy

sad

little

a big pig

a thin pig

a little pig

Match them!

Match the words to the pictures.
Begin like this:

five brown deer

one big bear

three fat rabbits

four green crocodiles

two happy lambs

six little owls

Match the sentences to the pictures.

Begin like this:

It is a little red ladybird.

It is a happy brown cow.

It is a big yellow camel.

It is a sad green frog.

It is a fat blue bird.

It is a thin pink pig.

Where do they live?

Which animals belong on the farm?
Match them to the picture.

cow

hen

kangaroo

pig

crocodile

horse